D0821793

Green Berets

BY LINDA BOZZO

amicus high interest

Amicus High Interest is an imprint of Amicus
P.O. Box 1329, Mankato, MN 56002
www.amicuspublishing.us

Library of Congress Cataloging-in-Publication Data
Bozzo, Linda.
 Green Berets / by Linda Bozzo.
     pages cm. – (Serving in the military)
 Includes index.
 Summary: "An introduction to the life of Green Berets in the
US Army Special Operations Command (USASOC) describing
some missions, how they train, and their role in the armed
forces"– Provided by publisher.
 ISBN 978-1-60753-492-1 (library bound)
 ISBN 978-1-60753-635-2 (ebook)
 1. United States. Army. Special Forces–Juvenile literature. I.
Title.
 UA34.S64B6579 2015
 356'.1670973–dc23
                                        2013039230

Editor: Wendy Dieker
Series Designer: Kathleen Petelinsek
Book Designer: Steve Christensen
Photo Researcher: Kurtis Kinneman

Photo Credits: Leif Skoogfors/Corbis, cover; imagebroker.net/
Superstock 5; David Leeson/Dallas Morning News/Sygma/
Corbis 6; pa european pressphoto agency b.v./Alamy 9; US
Marines Photo/Alamy 10; US Army Photo/Alamy 13; UK
MOD Image/Alamy 14; Rob Howard/CORBIS 17; Stocktrek
Images/Stocktrek Images/Corbis 18; Stocktrek Images/
Stocktrek Images/Corbis 21; Michael S. Yamashita/Corbis 22;
imagebroker.net/Superstock 25; Roger Arnold/Alamy 26; US
Navy Photo/Alamy 29

Printed in the United States at Corporate Graphics in North
Mankato, Minnesota.

10 9 8 7 6 5 4 3 2 1

Table of Contents

A War Hero

Captain Kent Solheim is a Green Beret. His team's job is to catch a **terrorist** leader in Iraq. It is the dark of night. His team fast-ropes from a chopper. Bang! Bang! Shots are fired! Solheim and his team charge around a corner. The team comes face-to-face with enemies.

Soldiers fast-rope from a chopper at night. They hope they aren't seen.

A nighttime gun battle is dangerous. Green Berets are ready to shoot at all times.

Solheim wants to save his men. He calls in
more soldiers. But he must charge ahead.
He is just in time! He shoots the enemy
fighter. The man falls to ground. But the
enemy is able to shoot his gun one last
time. Solheim is shot!

One bullet hits Solheim in the shoulder. Another goes through his left knee. Two more go through his right knee. But his team is saved.

When his team gets home, Solheim gets an award. He is awarded a Silver Star. He is a hero!

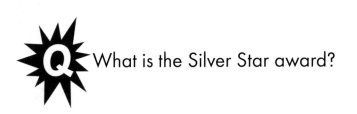
What is the Silver Star award?

At an awards ceremony,
Army Special Forces soldiers
wear green berets.

It is a medal given for bravery in combat.
It is the third-highest award given to soldiers.

Special Training

Green Berets are really called the U.S. Army Special Forces. Green Berets is a nickname. It comes from the hat they wear. These men have years of army training. But to become a Green Beret, a soldier needs even more training.

Soldiers train more for unsafe missions.

11

Soldiers start by getting ready for hard training. Men take a prep course to get fit. Next, they take the hardest training they will face: the SFAS. It is 24 days long. Soldiers march long distances with heavy loads. They run drills on obstacle courses. They take written tests. There is no time to relax. Only the best will make it through.

Q What does SFAS stand for?

Soldiers carry a heavy log as part of the training.

 It stands for Special Forces Assessment and Selection. Leaders watch and choose the best soldiers to be Green Berets.

Soldiers must learn a lot to pass each test. They work very hard.

 How many Green Berets are there?

Those who pass move on to qualification courses. There are five parts. Soldiers need to pass all of them to become Green Berets. In these parts, soldiers learn to work in small teams. They learn a new language, such as French or Arabic. They learn to survive anywhere in the world.

 Only about 4,500 men are Green Berets. That's only 1 percent of the U.S. Army.

Only the best soldiers pass the training courses. But the new Green Berets keep training. They learn the **cultures** of people in other countries. This helps them on missions.

These men keep practicing their fighting skills. They practice **close combat**. They keep their shooting skills sharp. Training never stops.

Green Berets go to sniper school. They practice shooting at targets far away.

These men use satellite radio gear to spy on enemies.

The Home Front

On the home front, Green Berets spy on the enemy. They help find clues about plans for attacks on the United States. This helps to stop attacks before they happen. The CIA or FBI might call on them for help. Protecting our country is a big part of the job.

When Green Berets come home from a mission, they still train. They get ready for the next fight. Each team prepares for their special job. A new mission could be in a different country. This means learning another language. A country with a different climate means learning new skills.

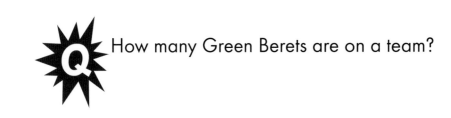 How many Green Berets are on a team?

Some teams practice shooting
when they are at home.

The Green Berets often work in 12-man
teams. They are called A-teams.

Overseas

The Green Berets are often the first ones sent on secret missions. They travel by land, air, or sea. They may spend periods of time behind enemy lines. Green Berets quietly spy on the enemy. They gather facts. This helps to plan their strike.

Men hide in the brush to spy.

Strikes are quick. A team will destroy enemy **weapons**. They **raid** enemy camps. They clear roadside bombs. They also work to save people who are in trouble.

Green Berets use special equipment on these strikes. They use **satellites**, radios, and computers to talk to each other.

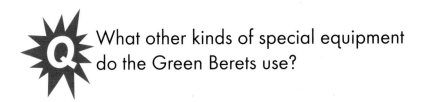

Q What other kinds of special equipment do the Green Berets use?

A scope like this helps soldiers see in dark places.

 Green Berets use Night Vision Goggles (NVGs) to see in the dark.

Green Berets teach soldiers in other countries.

Green Berets train soldiers in **ally countries**. They set up training camps. They teach the soldiers how to fight. They also teach them how to care for wounded soldiers. Trained soldiers around the world help protect both their country and ours.

Serving Our Country

The Green Berets are heroes. They keep the enemy from getting power in other countries. This helps protect our country from terror. They save our people trapped behind enemy lines. The Green Berets serve our country by getting the job done.

Green Berets are ready for any kind of mission.

Glossary

ally countries Countries that are friendly and help each other in time of trouble.

close combat Fighting between two or more people in a close range.

culture Everyday life of the people in a certain country.

raid A sudden and quick attack.

satellite A piece of equipment in space used to spy on enemies.

terrorist A person who uses attacks to cause fear.

weapon An object used in a fight to attack or defend.

Read More

Besel, Jennifer M. *The Green Berets.* Mankato, Minn: Capstone Press, 2011.

David, Jack. *Army Green Berets.* Minneapolis: Bellwether Media, 2009.

Hamilton, John. *United States Green Berets.* Edina, Minn.: ABDO, 2012.

Websites

Army Special Forces: Mission and History
www.military.com/special-operations/ army-special-forces-missions-and-history.html

Joining the Army Special Forces
www.military.com/special-operations/ joining-the-army-special-forces.html

U.S. Army Special Forces | goarmy.com
www.goarmy.com/special-forces.html

Index

About the Author

Linda Bozzo is the author of more than 45 books for the school and library market. She would like to thank all of the men and women in the military for their outstanding service to our country. Visit her website at www.lindabozzo.com.